Walther Ziegler

Rousseau
in 60 Minutes

Translated by
Alexander Reynolds

My thanks go to Rudolf Aichner for his tireless critical editing; Silke Ruthenberg for the fine graphics; Lydia Pointvogl, Eva Amberger, Christiane Hüttner, and Dr. Martin Engler for their excellent work as manuscript readers and sub-editors; Prof. Guntram Knapp, who first inspired me with enthusiasm for philosophy; and Angela Schumitz, who handled in the most professional manner, as chief editorial reader, the production of both the German and the English editions of this series of books.

My special thanks go to my translator

Dr Alexander Reynolds.

Himself a philosopher, he not only translated the original German text into English with great care and precision but also, in passages where this was required in order to ensure clear understanding, supplemented this text with certain formulations adapted specifically to the needs of English-language readers.

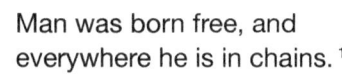

Bibliographic Information held by the German National Library: The details of the original German edition of this publication are held by the German National Library as part of the German National Bibliography; detailed bibliographical data can be found online at www.dnb.de.

© 2016 Dr Walther Ziegler
1st Edition June 2016
Jacket design and graphic design for the whole book: Silke Ruthenberg, making use of illustrations by:
Raphael Bräsecke, Creactive – Studio for Advertising, Comics & Illustrations
© JackF - Fotolia.com (image-frames)
© Valerie Potapova - Fotolia.com (image-frames)
© Svetlana Gryankina - Fotolia.com (speech-balloons)

Publisher and Printing:
BoD – Books on Demand, Norderstedt
ISBN 9783741227622

Contents

Rousseau's Great Discovery   7

Rousseau's Central Idea   15
- The Noble Savage   15
- Marriage and Language as Forms of Decadence   20
- The Curse of Settled Existence   25
- Living Outside Oneself   28
- The Lie of Property   32
- The State as Instrument for Repressing the Propertyless   34
- Back to Nature?   40
- The Social Contract as Solution   45
- The "General Will" and the "Will of All"   54
- Education in the Service of Man's Natural Freedom   65

Of What Use Is Rousseau's Discovery for Us Today?   73
- The Virtue of 'Contrariness' – Going One's Own Way   73
- Liberty, Equality and Fraternity!   77
- Daring More Democracy   80
- Mindfulness of Nature – Living Ecologically   83
- Educating Man to be Free   88
- Escaping the 'Matrix' – Living with Intensity   91

Bibliographical References   99

Rousseau's Great Discovery

Rousseau (1712-1778) was the most "contrary" of the world's great thinkers. He spoke and wrote against almost everything that his 18th-Century contemporaries held to be true and right: the divine right of kings, a society led by the aristocracy, the church, authoritarian education, and the state along with all its institutions.

He was the first really radical social critic. All his life he "swam against the current". Even today his work is anathema to many. Although Rousseau earned his living as a philosopher, artist and man of the theatre, he saw no contradiction in criticizing philosophy, art and the theatre as things that distracted from, and blinded to, the truth. He also had much to say on the topic of raising and teaching the young. He opposed to the methods of strict discipline current in the schools of his day an ideal of children's free self-development, founding a whole tradition of anti-authoritarian education.

His critique of all forms of repression and his political demand for democracy and equality prepared the ground for the French Revolution and inspired early socialism, Marxism and such later left-wing movements as Critical Theory. But many other apparently opposed movements of thought – such as the Sturm und Drang and Romantic movements or the philosophy of Nietzsche – were also influenced by Rousseau. This maverick thinker, in short, left no European thinker, of his own or later eras, indifferent. The stimuli he gave to posterity proved as diverse and as turbulent as the life he lived. No other philosopher, indeed, has left us a biography so rich in adventures and misfortunes.

When his restless life ended at the age of 66 he had practiced some twelve different professions, changed his religion twice, and adopted citizenship of three different nations. He had also set up house in a score of different locations and engaged in love affairs to a number which remains indeterminate but was certainly considerable.

Rousseau was also, however, a virtuoso of disaster and discord who somehow managed to quarrel with almost everyone who ever befriended or supported him. He made enemies, at one point or another, of Voltaire as well as of Diderot, D'Alembert and the other Encyclopédistes – men who had early on been his friends and allies – and even, finally, of the equable English philosopher David Hume who gave him shelter when his writings had forced him to seek refuge in England.

Rousseau, indeed, spent most of his life as a homeless wanderer or a hunted exile. He was persecuted and pursued sometimes by the church, sometimes by the government of one or another nation. At one point, with warrants for his arrest issued by both the republican government of his native Geneva and the parliament of his adopted France, he even took Prussian citizenship, i.e. that of the little Swiss principality of Neuchâtel ruled at the time by that patron of the Enlightenment, Prussia's Frederick the Great.

During his years of wandering he muddled through as a music teacher, a domestic, a house tutor, a lawyer's clerk, and a musical copyist, while sometimes pursuing his various actual vocations as novelist, philosopher and man of the theatre and opera, but never earned enough money to set up a household of his own. Still, he proved himself a real jack-of-all-trades. Some of his projects, indeed – such as his proposed new system of numbered musical notation – were failures. But his philosophical books and his novels were, many of them, European sensations and even his operas and theatrical pieces were appreciated and widely performed in his lifetime.

His mother died just a few days after his birth. His father raised him alone, giving him a first acquaintance with literature, but was obliged to leave Geneva after a quarrel with an officer who accused him of having drawn his sword on him, so that, from the age of ten on, Rousseau was cared for rather by his uncle, who apprenticed him to an engraver. At the age of sixteen, however, returning late from a Sunday outing and finding the city gates locked, Rousseau decided, rather than suffer a beating for his tardiness from his master, to leave Geneva forever and to seek his fortune in the world. For several years, he became a homeless wanderer in this corner of Europe where Switzerland borders Italy and France, earning a precarious living by odd jobs. But, being a handsome youth and already an engaging raconteur, he was usually able to find food and shelter on the lands of the region's various noblemen and -women. One such local noblewoman, Madame de Warens, even took him as a lover, although he continued all his life to refer to this benefactress, who was twelve years his elder, as his 'Mama'. Indeed, even after becoming a European celebrity, Rousseau continued to find benefactors and supporters among the nobility, such as Madame d'Épinay, who became his lover some years later. He spent, in fact, the greater part of his life as a guest at various courts and stately homes, even though his books preached social equality and the abolition of the aristocracy.

But such contradictions were very much a part of Rousseau's life. They did not prevent him from sometimes acting on firm principle. King Louis XV of France was so pleased with his opera *Le Devin du Village* that he was about to offer him a life pension – which Rousseau refused, however, despite his extreme poverty, because, as he wrote, to accept it would have been to say adieu to independence and freedom of speech – even about the king.

One of the few elements of constancy in Rousseau's life was, in fact, his long relationship with a woman from the other end of the social scale, the washerwoman Thérèse Le Vasseur, whom he finally married at age 56, ten years before his death, after having already given her five children. But here too Rousseau lived deep in self-contradiction, because he handed all these children over to a home for foundlings – a course of action unusual, to say the least, for the author of a much-praised work on child-care and education (the famous *Emile*, still today a point of reference for pedagogues). When Voltaire (still a friend at the time) asked him to explain this contradiction he replied that, as a writer, he simply did not have the time nor the money to raise children; just because he knew how much personal attention was needed to properly raise a child, he could not accept the responsibility involved in keeping them, and nor could his wife, since it was her work as a washerwoman that supported both him and herself. Although Rousseau's notoriously bad financial state lends a degree of credibility to this explanation, it still remains bizarre that a man who was looked up to by all Europe as a groundbreaking educationalist refused to raise or educate his own children. But Rousseau was not a practical man. He was a free spirit – a bold and uncompromising soul in the sphere of thought even if not always in that of action.

His most decisive thought – the one which, by his own account, changed his life forever and formed the core of his philosophy – was one which came to him only when he was almost forty years old, when he was on his way to visit his friend Diderot, who was being held in the prison at Vincennes for publishing views held to be seditious by the French monarchy. On the long walk to Vincennes he used to read the newspaper *Mercure de France*. One day, he happened to read in it of an essay competition, organized by the Dijon Academy, which invited the paper's readers to try to answer the question: "Has the restoration of the sciences and arts contributed to the purification of morals?", the best answer to receive a cash prize. The Academy received, as it had expected, overwhelmingly affirmative answers to this question. Rousseau alone thought to answer the question with a clear "no". Pondering this question, he had something like a supernatural experience, a kind of illumination, which made him thenceforth a profound sceptic regarding "the progress of civilization". He described this experience, in a letter to a friend, as follows:

> Suddenly I felt my mind dazzled by a thousand lights […]. A violent palpitation oppresses me, makes me sick to my stomach. Not being able to breathe any more while walking, I let myself fall under one of the trees of the avenue […]. Oh sir, if I had ever been able to write a quarter of what I saw and felt under that tree, how clearly I would have made all the contradictions of the social system seen; with what strength I would have exposed all the abuses of our institutions; with what simplicity I would have demonstrated that Man is naturally good and that it is from these institutions alone that men become wicked. [2]

But despite Rousseau's complaint here that he was unable to record but a few of the thoughts that came to him during this illumination, he can certainly be said to have seized and set down the key idea. Our civilization – such is Rousseau's central theme – has not led, as is generally believed, from savagery to order and from barbarism to law and morality but rather from an original simple beauty to decay and decadence:

Our souls have become corrupted in proportion as our sciences and arts have advanced toward perfection. [3]

Man, he wrote in the essay he submitted for the prize offered by the Dijon Academy, is by nature good and has become wicked only as a result of society and civilization. This unexpected and provocative thesis won him the prize. His essay, moreover, was published as a book, making him famous all over Europe overnight.

Rousseau's Central Idea

The Noble Savage

A few years later Rousseau tried to follow up this initial success by taking part in another "prize essay" competition organized by the Dijon Academy. This time he answered the question: 'What is the origin of inequality among people?' He took a similar culture-critical line as in his first essay: inequality, he argued, was likewise a result of civilization. At the dawn of history everyone had been equal and the fruits of the earth had belonged equally to all.

Then there had been no private property, neither palaces nor hovels, and thus no such thing as "rich" or "poor". In this "state of Nature", Rousseau argued, human beings roamed the forests as hunters and gatherers, seeking their subsistence. Such a lifestyle meant that they suffered neither from greed, egotism, envy nor morbid ambition. Man in this "state of Nature" lived a balanced life guided by healthy instincts, taking each day as it came with stoic equanimity:

> Accustomed from infancy to the inclemencies of the weather and the rigours of the seasons, used to fatigue and forced to defend themselves and their prey naked and unarmed against other wild beasts or to escape from them by running faster than they, men develop a robust and almost immutable constitution. ⁴

Hunting and fleeing from wild beasts and living in the open, these early human beings were also physically tough and fit, enjoying great health and beauty. They knew none of the diseases that come with civilization and prosperity, such as obesity or circulation problems. The superior health and beauty of these "noble savages" could, Rousseau argued, be deduced from the present appearance of such primitive peoples as the American Indians:

> When we think of the good constitution of savages – at least of those we have not corrupted with our strong liquors

– and reflect that they have almost no disorders except wounds and old age, we are almost prompted to believe that we could write the history of human illness by following the history of civilized societies. [5]

But the "noble savage", Rousseau went on, displayed not just a superior physique to the modern man but also a superior character. These "savages" each made their way through the forests alone and thus were unconcerned about their appearance:

[...] They had no kind of intercourse with one another, and had in consequence no experience of vanity, consideration, esteem or contempt [...]. They had not the least idea of 'mine' and 'yours'. [6]

Solitude, then, preserved early Man from that vanity which plagues his modern counterpart. Nonetheless, this primitive hunter and gatherer was already capable of empathy. He was, indeed, concerned first and foremost to preserve his own life – possessing as he did a healthy "love of self" (*amour de soi*) – but fellow feeling was also part of his nature:

There is [...] a principle which [...] serves to moderate the ardour he has for his own wellbeing by giving him an innate repugnance against seeing a fellow creature suffer. [7]

These "beautiful savages" in their "state of Nature", then, already display, for Rousseau, at least one innate virtue:

> I speak of compassion, a disposition well suited to creatures (like us) […] and a virtue all the more universal, and all the more useful to man, in that it comes before any kind of reflection. [8]

But the natural balance between feeling for others and love of oneself becomes lost in the process of civilization. Because life in cities causes the solitary savage's natural and healthy *amour de soi* to give way to *amour propre*, a much more artificial and unhealthy form of obsession with one's own person which had already been critically analysed at length by the French *philosophes* of the century preceding Rousseau. The "noble savage"'s "love of self" had merely been a concern for his own survival. But the "love of self" characteristic of dwellers in great modern cities, who mostly have all we need to survive, is something far worse: an urge to compare ourselves with others and to have more than they do, however much they have. In this way, we become greedy, envious and morbidly ambitious.

Marriage and Language as Forms of Decadence

In the "state of Nature" the institution of marriage was also unknown. How, asks Rousseau, could human beings in this natural state swear eternal fidelity before an altar when they had no words and no language? Instead, there existed a kind of "free love":

> As males and females united fortuitously according to encounters, opportunities and desires, they required no speech to express the things they had to say to each other and they separated with the same ease. [9]

Since in the "state of Nature" a man and a woman tended to go their separate ways right after performing the act of love, the question arises of how the resulting children were raised. Rousseau assumes that women could handle this task alone. He stresses the great independence that characterized these beautiful savages. Relationships of any duration were at this time an unnatural thing, since sexual pleasure tends to fade and these early human beings did not distinguish between sex and love, dalliance and marriage:

> (These men's experience was) confined solely to the physical part of love (and they were) fortunate enough to be ignorant of those preferences which stimulate the appetite while increasing the difficulties of satisfying it […]. [10]

Rousseau is thus strongly opposed to the theory propounded by John Locke whereby, in both man and animal, there is a natural inclination for both sexes to share the raising of the young until these latter are able to feed themselves. No such inclination, he argues, could possibly have developed in the "state of Nature", since the sexual act revealed its consequences only months later when the partners had gone their separate ways:

> His appetite satisfied, the man has no longer any need for a particular woman, nor the woman for a particular man [...]. One goes off in one direction, the other in another and there is no likelihood that at the end of nine months either will remember having known the other. [11]

Conjugal love, then, is for Rousseau something artificial, a construction of civilization. What we call "marriage" today Rousseau considered to be a clever and cunning invention of women aimed at controlling and dominating men:

> Now it is easy to see that the moral part of love is an artificial sentiment [...] cultivated by women with much skill and care in order

Rousseau's Central Idea

to establish their empire over men and so make dominant the sex that ought to obey. This sentiment [...] must be for (the savage) non-existent. [12]

Since the savage had, as yet, no ideal of beauty, the choice of a partner was not really a matter of taste; early human beings were not choosy about their lovers:

(The savage) responds only to the temperament which Nature has implanted in him and not to taste, which he has not been able to acquire: for him every woman is good. [13]

But a series of natural catastrophes, along with the steady growth in population, saw to it that these savages encountered each other more and more often and eventually formed permanent groups. This in turn led to the emergence of language, reflection and thereby also of philosophy. Rousseau looks on these developments as decadent: a very regrettable loss of the healthy instincts that had guided early Man as they still do animals:

I would almost venture to assert that the state of reflection is a state contrary to Nature and that the man who meditates is a depraved animal. [14]

But the process of society's formation could no longer be halted; the "beautiful savage" left his forests and wildernesses and founded, with others of his kind, the first permanent settlements.

The Curse of Settled Existence

But why did primitive human beings first join together into hordes and tribes if, as Rousseau claims, they were much happier in their original state as "lone wolves"? The answer is interesting: Man has a natural instinct to improve and perfect himself; therefore, he attempts to make his day-to-day existence ever more comfortable. It is this urge toward greater and greater comfort that eventually drives human beings out of the forests into permanent settlements. Since nights in the open air were often cold and rainy, early Man first sought shelter in caves and under trees. But at some point this was not enough for them and they became inventive:

> Soon [...] men discovered that various sorts of hard sharp stones could serve as hatchets to cut wood, dig the soil and make huts out of branches, which they learned to cover with clay and mud.

> This was the epoch of a first revolution, which established and differentiated families and which introduced property of a sort from which perhaps even then many quarrels and fights were born. [15]

But hardly had the "noble savages" left their forests and begun to build permanent homes than quarrels began over whose hut or cottage would be the finest. The next step toward civilization was the introduction of agriculture and cattle-rearing. Here too, says Rousseau, it was a concern for comfort that prompted mankind to quit the "state of Nature". Instead of having, as hunters and gatherers, to chase down animals or scour the woodland floors for fruit, they now bred and raised the animals they ate and grew the fruit directly before their own doors. But mankind paid a high price for such comfort:

> [...] Vast forests were transformed into pleasant fields which had to be watered with the sweat of men, and where slavery and misery were soon seen to germinate and flourish with the crops. [16]

Farming fields and storing the crops away was a securer way of life, indeed, than hoping for luck in the hunt. But for men to work to a routine and to dwell together in farmsteads and villages meant that people gradually separated out into landowning farmers and landless farm-labourers. The naturally-existing freedom and equality of mankind was destroyed. Suddenly, there were "eminent men" and men less eminent.

In the "state of Nature" no such hierarchy had been possible, since each hunter or gatherer had roamed naked and alone through the forests. The idea of a "yours" and a "mine" – i.e. the sense of being a "man of property" or a "poor devil" – emerged, claims Rousseau, only with agriculture.

Living Outside Oneself

Life in fixed settlements also brought a further problem. People now lived close together and celebrated festivals in common but even this had fateful consequences:

> People grew used to gathering together in front of their huts or around a large tree […]. Each began to look at the others and to want to be looked at himself, and public esteem came to be prized. He who sang or danced the best; he who was the most handsome, the strongest, the most adroit or the most elegant became the most highly regarded, and this was the first step toward inequality and at the same time toward vice. [17]

With song, speech and thought came conventional forms of interaction. People began to say "please" and "thank you" and to address one another by fixed titles

– something the "noble savage" would have found incomprehensible. These fixed forms of interaction became more and more refined until there emerged what we call "politeness", "etiquette" and "good manners". The "noble savage"'s anger or joy could be easily read from his face. When two such early men met in the forest each could instantly tell whether the other was hostile, friendly or afraid. Spontaneity and uninhibitedness were the rule because each was a "lone wolf" who hearkened only to his own mood. But as culture progresses, says Rousseau, this wonderful idiosyncrasy of each individual is completely lost:

Today [...] a vile and deceitful uniformity reigns in our mores and all minds seem to have been cast in the same mould. Without ceasing, politeness makes demands, propriety gives orders; without ceasing, common customs are followed, never one's own lights. [18]

Such a total adaptation of human beings to conventions leads to a growing loss of identity. Each one learns to practice disguise and deceit and tends to assume (usually rightly) that the other person is being deceitful too:

> One no longer dares to seem what one really is. And in this perpetual restraint the men who make up this herd we call society [...] do all the same things [...]. Thus no one will ever really know those with whom he is dealing. [19]

Since each wants to make a good impression on others, he engages only in that behaviour that will, as he thinks, please others most:

> The savage lives within himself; social man lives always outside himself; he knows how to live only in the opinion of others;

it is, so to speak, from their judgment alone that he derives the sense of his own existence. [20]

This constant orientation toward how others see him may indeed make the individual applauded and admired. But the price of this "role-playing" is the loss of all naturalness.

The Lie of Property

Rousseau particularly condemns, as the most fateful moment in human history, the seizure of land by the first settled farmers. His description of how property first arose is still often quoted even today:

> The first man who, having enclosed a piece of land, thought of saying 'This is mine' and found people simple enough to believe him was the true founder of civil society. How many crimes, wars, murders; how much misery and horror the human race would have been spared if someone had pulled up the stakes and filled in the ditch and cried to his fellow men: 'Beware of listening to this impostor! You are lost if you forget that the fruits of the earth belong to everyone and that the earth itself belongs to no one! [21]

Rousseau's Central Idea

Because the emergence of private property split humanity into classes: into rich and poor, "haves" and "have nots", revealing itself to be the main cause of all modern vices. With the birth of property there was also born envy, resentment and shame on the side of the poor and greed, overweening pride and contempt on the side of the rich. Each man wanted the biggest house, the finest estate, or the largest number of factories. There began a limitless competition for goods and fine appearances. Ever since there has been property, says Rousseau, all have been trying "to make their fortune at others' cost". None of this could have happened in the "state of Nature", since the "noble savage" had neither known property nor desired it:

His desires do not go beyond his physical needs; the only good things he knows in the universe are food, a female, and repose; and the only evils he fears are pain and hunger. [22]

With the introduction of property came luxury for the few, but for many lifelong oppression.

The State as Instrument for Repressing the Propertyless

At first, those who had succeeded in fencing off a piece of earth and becoming landowners were hardly able to enjoy their property. They lived constantly in fear of a stronger man's coming to steal their harvest or even to drive them off their property forever. Rousseau portrays the struggle of the earliest settlers and cattle-farmers for farming and grazing land as a very violent one that required each settler to be ready to fight:

> There arose between the right of the stronger and the right of the first occupant a perpetual conflict which ended only in fights and murders. [23]

Not even a physically strong landowner skilled in the use of weapons could feel safe, because the landless and hungry often acted in unison:

> The rich man was now [...] under pressure of necessity [...] and alone against all [...]. [24]

So as to end this constant insecurity, the rich founded states in which they would no longer have to personally defend their own pieces of land with clubs or other weapons but could leave this dangerous work to the police. In place of that "might is right" which had been the law of the "state of Nature", the emerging rich put a new artificial law that met their need for protection. The state, with its laws and judges, was an ideal way for the rich man to stay unmolested by the poor. In order to persuade the poor to permit this, of course, the rich man had to apply many tricks and rhetorical inventions:

But since human beings in this period of the first foundation of the world's states were still very naïve, they believed these rich men's promises and consented. There arose a whole series of states, smaller and larger. For Rousseau, this signified a legalization of the violent seizure of land and a definitive dispossession of the poor:

Rousseau's Central Idea

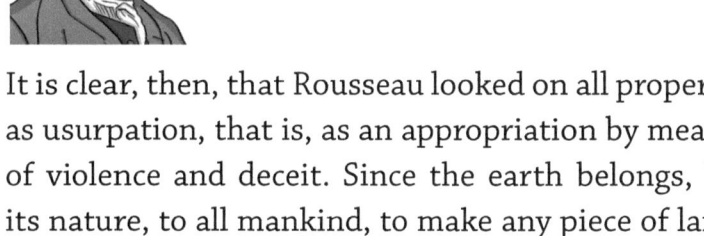

(Society and laws) put new fetters on the weak and gave new powers to the rich, which irretrievably destroyed natural liberty, established for all time the law of property and inequality, and transformed adroit usurpation into irrevocable right. [26]

It is clear, then, that Rousseau looked on all property as usurpation, that is, as an appropriation by means of violence and deceit. Since the earth belongs, by its nature, to all mankind, to make any piece of land one's own is always to act unjustly.

Once states had been founded, then, with their policemen, judges and prison warders, the liberty and equality of human beings was a thing of the past. Through settled living, agriculture, property, speech, marriage and the state civilization gradually enslaved the "noble savage". The characters of all men, even of the rich, suffered harm from this development. Even those who stand, as men of eminence and repute, at the very summit of the state are, says Rousseau, only pitiful examples of a degenerate species. Thus he compares the daily routine of a plump government minister, sitting all day at his desk in wig and tailcoat, with that of a muscular Caribbean islander, clad only in a loincloth, climbing palm trees to pluck coconuts:

> What a spectacle for a Carib would be the arduous and envied labours of a European minister! How many cruel deaths would not that indolent savage prefer to the horrors of such a life […]. 27

The "indolent savage" and the minister, he goes on, are as different in their mentalities as they are in their outward appearance:

> The savage man breathes only peace and freedom; he desires only to live and stay idle […]. Civil man, on the contrary, being

Rousseau´s Central Idea

always active, sweating and restless, torments himself endlessly in search of ever more laborious occupations. He works himself to death [...] to live. [28]

Back to Nature?

This, then, is Rousseau's central idea. It is only through civilization that Man becomes wicked. By nature, he is healthy, guided by sound instincts and moral:

> We conclude, then, that savage man, wandering in the forests [...] without speech, without a home, without war and without relationships, was equally without need of his fellow men and without any desire to hurt them [...]. He felt only his true needs. [29]

By contrast to this "noble savage", the self-seeking modern city-dweller cannot even recognize what his real needs are. The modern "bourgeois" is not content to live for himself but lives rather only under, and through, the gaze of others, struggling hectically all his life for money, honour and power.

In sum, then, Rousseau found mankind to have been following, for many hundreds of years, a fundamentally wrong path. When Rousseau sent a copy of his essay on *The Origins of Inequality* to his older contemporary, the great Voltaire, the older man responded with a letter written in his characteristic tone of dry but biting wit: "I have received, sir, your new book against the human species [...]. No one has ever been so witty as you are in trying to turn us into brutes. To read your book makes one long to go on all fours."[30]

The potential for discord between the two great writers which is clear already in this letter of 1755 soon developed to such a point that, in a letter of 1760, Rousseau wrote to Voltaire words that made reconciliation impossible:

I love you not, sir [...]. Rather, I hate you, since you have been desirous that I should. [31]

Voltaire thereupon broke off all contact with the younger man, writing to their mutual acquaintance D'Alembert that Rousseau had "completely lost his mind". But, insofar as the roots of this quarrel can be traced back to Voltaire's sarcastic lines of 1755 regarding Rousseau's essay on *The Origins of Inequality*, Rousseau's annoyance is, in fact, understandable. Voltaire had clearly deliberately misrepresented Rousseau's critique of civilization in saying that it "made the reader long to go on all fours." Rousseau, of course, had not been so naïve as to believe that mankind could simply retreat back into the "state of Nature". That he knew that this is impossible is clear from what he says when he writes:

> What then? Must we destroy societies, annihilate 'mine' and 'yours' and return to live in the forests with the bears?
>
> A conclusion in the style of my adversaries, which I would sooner forestall than permit them to disgrace themselves by drawing. [32]

Rousseau goes on to state that it is impossible for Man to begin once again "to live on herbs and acorns". His philosophical vision is rather one of individuals' turning away, even within modern civilized society, from the restlessness that characterizes this society, by becoming mindful of virtue and of the values of the heart. One finds, in fact, nowhere in Rousseau the famous phrase "Back to Nature!" that is so often ascribed to him. Because he knew very well that "there is no going back". Indeed, his hypothesis concerning the "noble savage" and this latter's unspoiled character in the "state of Nature" was not a real historical claim at all, but just that: a hypothetical construction. Rousseau himself admits that the thoughts he expounds regarding the "state of Nature" are more an argumentational device than a description of fact.

> One must not take the kind of research which we enter into here as the pursuit of truths of history but solely as hypothetical and conditional reasonings, better fitted to clarify the nature of things than to expose their actual origin. [33]

Rousseau's key intention, then, was not to prove that mankind's history had unfolded in just the way he recounted it but simply to make the point that our modern world is by no means the best of all possible worlds and that not every "progress of civilization" really is the progress it purports to be. The "thought experiment" of the "state of Nature" really only serves as a platform from which Rousseau can name and criticize the failings of civilization:

> Men are wicked. […] Yet Man is naturally good; I believe I have demonstrated it. […] Admire human society as you will, it is nonetheless true that it necessarily leads men to hate each other in proportion to the extent that their interests conflict. [34]

But where do we go from here? What is to be done? The way back, clearly, is closed to us. Is there a way forward and out of our situation or will Man just continue to become more and more corrupt? Rousseau too asked himself the difficult question: can one live in a modern society yet still preserve the natural freedom and independence of the "state of Nature"? Rousseau gives a fascinating answer to this question in his much-discussed book *The Social Contract*.

The Social Contract as Solution

This famous book begins exactly where Rousseau's essay on *The Origin of Inequality* ends: namely, with the description of the contradictory state of our world:

Man was born free, and everywhere he is in chains. [35]

However, a just society, Rousseau argues, can never be built upon violence and the oppression of those without property but must rather respect the liberty of its members. How, though, can Man preserve his naturally good character, his liberty and his independence when he lives no longer in the forests as a "lone wolf" but rather in society with other people? Must he make compromises here? Rousseau formulates the search for an ideal society in the following terms:

> Find a form of association which will defend and protect, with the whole of its joint strength, the person and property of each associate and under which each of them, uniting himself to all, will obey himself alone, and remain as free as before. [36]

But what does such an association look like? If Man is to retain the independence and liberty he had enjoyed in the "state of Nature", then he cannot possibly submit to laws and judges, because his freedom is an essential part of his humanity and must remain sacrosanct. On the one hand, then, basic principle dictates that the individual's ceding of his right of self-determination to a king, a parliament or some other form of government is quite out of the question, something which Rousseau states clearly when he writes:

Rousseau's Central Idea

> To renounce our freedom is to renounce our character as men: (to renounce) the rights of humanity. [37]

On the other hand, though, if a state is to be established, each citizen must do precisely this – give up his right to self-determination – because when living in society one can clearly no longer simply follow one's spontaneous instincts and do whatever one wishes. One cannot, for example, take the law into one's own hands and avenge perceived wrongs oneself and one must, in general, follow society's rules. Rousseau was aware of this contradictory situation and applied his philosophical mind to resolving the contradiction, setting himself the task of designing a state that would ensure both the full liberty of the individual and a peaceful social coexistence.

His solution here is bewilderingly radical. He argues that there is only one form of state that can possibly fulfil both these contradictory requirements: namely, direct democracy. Each individual citizen must, even when he joins together with others to form a society, still stay, as in the "state of Nature", a ruler over his own self, able to freely decide his fate. In an ideal society, then, there can be no rulers and no ruled but only free citizens who rule themselves. There can be no king, prince or dictator. Nor can there be parties, parliamentary delegates or governments. No one but the assembly of all citizens – that is to say, the people itself – can have the right to pass laws, which will then be binding on all. Anything else, argues Rousseau, would mean citizens being ruled by a power that was not their own:

Any law that the people in person has not ratified is void. [38]

The citizen, then, submits only to those laws which he has made himself, of his own free will. Inasmuch as he is sovereign and subject at once, the will he obeys is his own, so that even in obeying, he is free. Rousseau sums this up in the pithy formula:

[...] to obey a law that we have imposed on ourselves is freedom. 39

But Rousseau must concede that there is an essential difference between the liberty of the citizen in the state and the absolute liberty of the "noble savage" in the "state of Nature". In society, the individual can no longer merely take whatever he wants:

What Man loses by the social contract is his natural freedom and an unlimited right to anything by which he is tempted and can obtain; what he gains is civil freedom and the right of property over everything he possesses. 40

This passage is interesting inasmuch as Rousseau here clearly admits that even in his ideal state there exists a right to private property. The citizen may keep what he possesses. This stands at odds with Rousseau's earlier thesis that property is, in principle, illegitimate appropriation.

It is surely for this reason that Rousseau specifies that strict limits must be set to property ownership and that the "social contract", while indeed securing the right to own property, implicitly also imposes on the property-owner a special obligation vis-à-vis society as a whole.

The "social contract" is thus the solution for the great problem posed by the natural liberty of the individual on the one hand and the necessity of subjection to law on the other. By being both sovereign and subject at once, an individual obeys no one but himself. His liberty is preserved. All those citizens who have entered into a "social contract" to establish a state gather in great assemblies and decide together on all the laws that they wish to give themselves. For such a design to function, the state in question would need, ideally, to be very small. Rousseau also emphasizes that these people's assemblies need to be held where all citizens can easily reach them and, moreover, at very frequent intervals:

Rousseau's Central Idea

> Apart from the extraordinary assemblies that may be required in unforeseen circumstances, there must be others, fixed at regular intervals, which nothing can abolish or postpone [...]. [41]

Rousseau's models for this ideal state included the plebiscites he knew from his native Switzerland and from his reading about the ancient Greek city-states. But in contrast to the ancient polis, Rousseau recommends that the citizens of the state described in his *Social Contract* elect no such statesmen as the great Pericles to "stand in" for them in the management of governmental affairs but rather decide all such matters themselves. He also considers parliamentary delegates and political parties to be dangerous, since they often have an eye not on the general welfare but on the interests of a specific group of voters:

> I therefore assert that sovereignty, being only the exercise of the general will, can never be transferred [...]. 42

This means, of course, that Rousseau rejects also our present-day parliamentary democracy. Only when citizens pass, themselves, the laws that are to apply to them do they remain truly free. And indeed it can be said that, as long as the votes that pass such laws are unanimous, each man submits only to a law he himself bears personal responsibility for. But how is it in the case where, at such a vote, one man is voted down by the majority?

> But the question is how a man can be free and forced to conform to the will of others than himself.

> How can those who are in opposition be free and subject to laws to which they have not consented? [43]

To deal with this question Rousseau adds an essential nuance to his model of direct-democratic plebiscites. These plebiscites must never merely be a matter of the majority's forcing its interest through against the minority. Rather, already prior to the vote, all participating citizens must have allowed the "general interest" to have stepped into the place of any individual interest. This brings us to the very core of Rousseau's model of democracy: his demand that the state realize the *volonté générale* or "general will".

The "General Will" and the "Will of All"

In a truly proper expression of a people's democratic will each citizen must entirely put aside his egotistical individual interest and make his choice solely with a view to the welfare of the entire community. If each individual, when voting in the assembly on a law, pursues only his own advantage, the end result of such a vote will be what Rousseau contemptuously calls the mere *volonté de tous*, or "will of all". A society founded only on such an egoistically-emerging "will of all" is typical of the corrupted modern world, described by Rousseau in his early essays, in which people inhabit a common space, such as a city, but think only of themselves. Rousseau's ideal state, though, aspires to something higher than this: a community of "citizens" (in the fuller sense of this term) who vote rather with a view to what is best for the commonweal to which they belong. It is only a vote in such a spirit that produces a *volonté générale*, or true "general will".

If, for example, there were a vote on the raising of the minimum wage for barbers, that an egoistic modern individual who is a mere "inhabitant" of the city he shares with others would vote against, for fear that a haircut could become more expensive for him personally. But the true citizen (in the fuller sense) of a city or city-state might vote to grant barbers a higher wage, prompted by the consideration that large differences in income endanger social harmony, so that his vote would be an expression of the general will, not just something randomly added to a cumulative "will of all".

Rousseau, of course, knew what a difficult demand is made on citizens when they are asked to put, in all their decisions, the interest of society as a whole above their own personal interest. If, for example, there were proposed in a Roussean popular assembly the siting of a rubbish dump just outside the city, it would clearly be no easy thing for a man who happened to live at just that spot to vote for such a proposition as something in the general interest:

For each individual can have, as a man, a personal will that is contrary or dissimilar to the general will that he has as a citizen. His personal interest can speak to him quite differently from the common interest. [44]

In such a case, indeed, the citizens' assembly might possibly look for some other site or pay the affected man some compensation. But even if both of these things prove, for one reason or another, impossible, the man who has been voted down must still abide by the law:

> In order, therefore, that the social pact should not be an empty formula, it contains an implicit obligation which alone can give force to the others: that if anyone refuses to obey the general will he will be compelled to do so by the whole body; which means nothing else but that he will be forced to be free. [45]

Rousseau's Central Idea

The more important a law is, says Rousseau, the harder the citizens' assembly must try to arrive at a unanimous decision. But in an emergency – when there is no time or unanimity proves impossible to achieve – even a mere majority decision must be accepted by all as the "general will", for:

> When a law is proposed in the assembly of the people, what they are asked is not precisely whether they accept or reject the proposal, but whether it is or is not in conformity with the general will, which is their will; everyone, by voting, gives his opinion on the question; and counting the votes makes the general will manifest. When an opinion contrary to mine prevails, therefore, it proves only that I had been mistaken and that the general will was not what I had believed it to be. [46]

Each citizen, then, must cast his vote in the spirit of the commonweal and accept the emerging result. The "general will" is thus infallible and the highest legislative and moral authority in society. For this reason no citizen may give, for example, priority to his religious convictions over the law. Rousseau advocates, indeed, religious tolerance, whereby each person may freely choose and practice his belief. But he must also respect those of different beliefs and above all respect the state. He proposes strict measures against religious fundamentalists:

But anyone who dares to say 'There is no salvation outside the Church' must be expelled from the state […]. [47]

Firm action must also be taken against egotistical citizens who fail to abide by the democratic laws of the citizens' assembly or consciously break them:

> Moreover, every wrongdoer, in attacking the rights of society by his crimes, becomes a rebel and a traitor to his country. By violating its laws he ceases to belong to it […]. But since he has acknowledged his membership (of the society and country), if only by his place of residence, he must be removed from it – by exile inasmuch as he has infringed the contract, or by death inasmuch as he is a public enemy. [48]

His recommending such radical action against citizens who place their personal welfare above the "general will", along with his thesis that this "general will" is infallible, have raised the question of whether Rousseau's *Social Contract* does not perhaps contain totalitarian elements.

Already in his lifetime Rousseau's *Social Contract* was the subject of discussion and controversy all across Europe. His works were read with enthusiasm not only by his immediate contemporaries but also by the next generation, which included Kant and Goethe, and the generation after that, which included Wordsworth and the other great Romantics. Between these two generations fell the birth of the man whose enthusiasm for Rousseau had perhaps the gravest historical consequences of all. Maximilien de Robespierre claimed to have made a personal visit to Rousseau in the philosopher's final days, when Robespierre himself was still a shy and puritanical law student, and to have sworn to him to put his ideals into practice. He got his chance to do so a dozen years later when revolution seized France and Robespierre swiftly rose from the position of delegate to the new-formed National Assembly to that of chairman of the much-feared Committee of Public Safety. As chairman of this committee and leader of the faction of the Jacobins, the once-introverted Robespierre was, for a few years, the most powerful man in France. In this position the moral puritanism he had carried over from his Roussean youth prompted him to establish a dictatorship of (what he perceived as) virtue that has gone down in history as "the Terror". He felt he had the right and even the duty to persecute all those French citizens who, in his view, opposed the "general will". He sent thousands into exile and many thousands more to the guillotine, citing in support of this Rousseau's recommended strictures against enemies of the state. In the end, he died on the guillotine himself.

It is in part due to historical developments like this that debate continues, still today, among political scientists as to whether Rousseau's claim that the state has the right to use coercive measures to make the individual citizen respect the "general will", may play into the hands of totalitarianism. Rousseau does indeed recommend that traitors, and citizens who place private interests above those of the nation-state, be severely punished:

> He can be banished, not for impiety, but for being unsociable, and for being incapable of cherishing the laws and justice sincerely, or of sacrificing, when necessary, his life for his duty. [49]

Is this demand that the citizen be prepared to sacrifice himself and submit himself to the "general will" a first step toward dictatorship? Or just a necessary measure in order to protect democracy from its "enemies within"?

The question is difficult to answer. On the one hand, Rousseau almost invites this charge of totalitarianism by suggesting that "enemies of the state" could even suffer the death penalty; on the other hand, he repeatedly emphasized that the "general will" can only emerge out of regular and frequent voting assemblies of the entire people and never out of the personal judgments of individual bearers of the people's mandate who may, like Robespierre, become blinded by power:

> If, therefore, the people simply promises to obey, it dissolves itself by this very act and loses its character as a people. From the moment that there is a master, sovereign authority ceases, and the body politic is thenceforward destroyed. [50]

Rousseau, then, was without a doubt a firm opponent of every kind of dictatorship and would certainly also have rejected the "Terror" presided over by Robespierre's Committee of Public Safety as undemocratic and criminal. It can be said, though, that his wish that citizens always place, in expressions of the popular will, the general good above their private interest appears to us today to be a somewhat utopian idea. Workers and employers, for instance, clearly have different interests so that, as modern critics of Rousseau have argued, there cannot, in a society based on competition, be such a thing as an objective "general will". It is indeed, such critics have insisted, important in a pluralistic society that the private interests of each social group be included in debates, so as to aid the search for sound compromises. Rousseau's demand that workers, for example, put aside their own interests for the sake of the "fatherland" or any such "common good" appears in this light not as a doctrine of virtue but, on the contrary, as a highly dangerous ideology.

In Rousseau's defence here it can be said that the world Rousseau lived in had hardly yet been touched by capitalism and that he had in mind, when he demanded that states realize the "common good", above all the oppression of the common people by the aristocracy. It must also not be forgotten that Rousseau was a convinced Enlightenment thinker and was thus always committed to tolerance as the basic doctrine of any future state:

> Now that there is no longer, and cannot be, an exclusive national religion, all those which tolerate other religions ought to be tolerated, to the extent that their dogmas contain nothing contrary to the duties of the citizen. [51]

It is also the case that Rousseau, with his radical demand for rule by the people as the only truly just form of government, inspired the French Revolution. He died eleven years too early to see how his *Social Contract* was used as a model in the formulation of the first French constitution. The famous slogan of the French republic *'liberté, égalité, fraternité'* is surely to be traced back to Rousseau's work. It is said that, when the deposed King Louis XVI found, in the prison where he was held, books by Rousseau and Voltaire, he cried out furiously: "These are the two men who have destroyed France!" Indeed, in preparing the way for the French Revolution Rousseau can be said to have prepared that of all modern Europe.

Education in the Service of Man's Natural Freedom

Besides his main political work, the *Social Contract*, Rousseau also authored a manifesto for a new sort of education. Here, he tried to revive and reinvigorate the natural liberty of human beings. Rousseau knew that there was no real way back into the "state of Nature". Civilization had already moved far too far away from its origin. Even the foundation of directly democratic republics such as he envisaged in the Social Contract could only remove some few special impositions of this civilization, such as political inequality. Nevertheless, Rousseau also saw a second great chance to free later generations from that social alienation that weighed on his own contemporaries: namely, a change in the way children were reared and educated.

He believed that it was possible, with a little skill, to raise children to be free and self-confident human beings even despite all the constraints of the property-based society they were born into. His idea was simple and consistent. A newborn child is, in his heart's core, always still a "noble savage", since he has, as yet, no idea of civilization. He "starts at zero", as it were, and is initially completely uncorrupted. And since this small human being is, by nature, good, with virtue tending to develop spontaneously in him, one need only allow this development to freely take its course. The main task of education is thus, for Rousseau, a passive or, as he himself puts it, a "negative" one:

Thus, the first education ought to be purely negative. It consists not at all in teaching virtue or truth but in securing the heart from vice and the mind from error. ⁵²

Any authoritarian indoctrination with social values or cultural knowledge would immediately corrupt the innocence of the child and is therefore inadmissible. "Raising" by parents must be replaced by a natural self-development on the part of the child.

Rousseau chose not to publish this new philosophy of education, as one might have expected, as a scientific textbook but rather in the form of a novel, entitled

Emile, or On Education. In this novel, Emile is the name given to a newborn child whose process of maturation, from birth to adulthood, is described in exciting detail. Rousseau uses this process to illustrate just what a proper education would look like. The main error, he contends, of traditional child-rearing has been that adults have always tried to raise children as they raise vegetables or fruit-trees subject to the farmer's manipulation and control:

> Everything is good as it leaves the hands of the Author of things; everything degenerates in the hands of Man. He forces one soil to nourish the products of another, one tree to bear the fruit of another [...]. He wants nothing as Nature made it, not even Man; for him, Man must be trained like a school horse; Man must be fashioned in keeping with his fancy like a tree in his garden. [53]

These opening sentences of *Emile* already set the direction in which a proper education must seek to exert its effects. It must not force or mould a child's nature but rather just let it flourish. Emile, therefore, is raised from the very start without any of the trappings the 18th Century usually laid on small children:

> Emile will not have padded bonnets, strollers, buggies or leading strings […]. 54

Nor is any over-protective nurse or nanny to be allowed to prevent the child's free self-development:

> Instead of letting him stagnate in the stale air of a room, let him be taken daily to the middle of a field. There let him run and frisk about; let him fall a hundred times a day. So much the better. That way he will learn to get up sooner. 55

Rousseau knew, of course, that one could not leave children completely unsupervised without running a risk that they would starve or otherwise come to harm. He proposed, therefore, in *Emile*, that all children be confided, for their first twelve years, to the care of a tutor, whose main task it would be to protect them from the influence of culture and to see that they are not corrupted by the influence either of their parents or of a formal schooling begun too early. Instead, the children should gather as many concrete experiences as possible and discover the world in their own way, obeying only their own curiosity and natural urge to be active:

> I cannot repeat too often that only physical objects can interest children [...]. All that depends on the moral order and on the practice of society ought not to be presented to them yet because they are not in a condition to understand it. [56]

Rousseau recommends here the use of a little trick:

> Let him always believe he is the master, and let it always be you who are. [57]

The tutor must, indeed, be in every respect a model of rectitude and virtue. He may, however, engage in a certain "role-play", so that control is maintained even while facilitating the child's free self-development:

> Doubtless he ought to do only what he wants, but he ought to want only what you want him to do. [58]

Emile learns a solid handicraft, being apprenticed to a carpenter. Only after completing his twelfth year is he really "socialized" and confronted with certain key mental and spiritual experiences. Here too, it is emotional development that is given pride of place. At an age where the sex-drive first awakens he is brought together with the peasant girl Sophie and experiences with her the feeling of loving affection. Only after this are certain abstract social norms and rules of conduct gradually taught to the now-pubescent boy.

Rousseau's philosophy of education is not free of contradictions and inconsistencies. Thus, Emile's first lover, Sophie, is not chosen by Emile himself but by his tutor – which appears to run counter to Rousseau's own demand that the young person be allowed to make his own choices. Rousseau's whole model, indeed, of a self-development shielded and cut off from human society appears highly questionable to us today. In Emile there is refused to the young protagonist every normal contact with parents or boys his own age but the pedagogical consensus today is that such early social contact is beneficial and even necessary.

All the same, Rousseau's idea of a non-authoritarian education that took into account the child's own urge to self-development was certainly an important new, indeed revolutionary, approach. Each small human being was to get the chance to discover the world for himself and to form and shape it according to his own needs and abilities. It is only so, thought Rousseau, that such a small human being can develop a healthy sense of self that allows him, later, to deal critically and constructively with the norms, rules of conduct and constraints of the society he grows up into. More than a century later Rousseau's views here received support from a rather different philosophical angle. Sigmund Freud's doctrine of psychoanalysis also lays emphasis on how children can be traumatized and permanently damaged by too strict a control of their natural impulses at too early an age.

Of What Use Is Rousseau's Discovery for Us Today?

The Virtue of 'Contrariness' – Going One's Own Way

There can be no doubt that Rousseau possessed a brilliant mind and one that questioned every accepted value and idea. Whatever most were "for", Rousseau was always "against". He was against monarchy, against the church, against the status quo, against inequality, against traditional education, against marriage, and (of course) against technical progress and the destruction of Nature. Today we might call Rousseau a "professional rabble-rouser". His "contrariness" was a kind of a trademark for him. He was aware of this himself from very early on in his career. Already in the introduction to his first "prize essay" he clearly distances himself from the way of thinking dominant in his age:

> There will always be men destined to be subjugated by the opinions of their century, their country, their society […]. One should not write for such readers when one wants to live beyond one's century. [59]

And Rousseau certainly did want to live beyond his century. He had a sense of a mission. His goal, immodest as it may sound, was the deconstruction of every idea and value that characterized his age. Here he left no moral or intellectual stone upon another.

His contemporaries believed that material progress would mean also mankind's moral improvement; Rousseau maintained the contrary. His fellow citizens looked on property as a natural and rightful inheritance; Rousseau saw it as injustice. To the pedagogues of the day children were deficient beings who needed to be made into adults as quickly as possible; for Rousseau the opposite was true. It is no wonder, then, that we find the advice given in his Emile:

Of What Use Is Rousseau's Discovery for Us Today?

> Take the opposite of the practiced path and you will almost always do well. [60]

He both gave and followed this advice in his own life. He not only rejected the customary white wigs, court soirées and other fashionable accessories of his age but urban living itself and even such a basic institution as marriage. He preferred to live in the country and sometimes, as in one famous portrait, wore the fur hat and kaftan of an Armenian peasant to set himself off, also externally, from the conforming bourgeois city-dwellers of his day.

Not even God was beyond his critical reach. He rejected not just the liturgy of the church but the very idea of a personal God as a Heavenly Father, defending rather the pantheistic view that God is present in all of Nature. One was closer to God, he said, in the forest than in any church or temple and could feel Him better in one's own inmost heart than in holy texts or vicars' sermons.

In short, Rousseau was a notorious contrarian who surely took a certain pleasure in "rubbing people (and ideas) the wrong way". It is no wonder, then, that he ended up turning everyone against him, even former allies and companions, and spent half his life fleeing warrants for his arrest for disobedience to church or state authorities. His native city of Geneva ended up ordering the burning of his books and even in the small Swiss town of Môtiers, where he took refuge, he had to flee outraged townspeople throwing stones at his windows.

Rousseau's biography and his work, then, are a timeless challenge to people to take a critical stance against the accepted truths and conventions of their respective ages. Often, new visions only emerge when one dares to confront and oppose what has been handed down for generations. Although Rousseau may have gone too far with some of his theses, his radicalism has inspired and stimulated many decisive developments during the two and a half centuries since his day.

Liberty, Equality and Fraternity!

There can be no doubt that Rousseau's work contains a social-revolutionary core. He very clearly questions the legitimacy of hereditary monarchy. Such famous sentiments of the French Revolution as "Who is to rule the people if not the people itself?" and "Liberty, equality and fraternity" can certainly be seen as effects, in the longer term, of Rousseau's ideas. Although he did not live to see the Revolution itself, the revolutionaries of 1789 and the years that followed honoured his memory highly. Sixteen years after his death his remains were transferred, amidst public celebrations, to Paris's newly-established "Pantheon", the great mausoleum for the national heroes of France.

The revolutionaries were right here inasmuch as, whereas even such mighty spirits as Voltaire, Kant and Hegel had continued to defend their kings and princes as legitimate rulers – either coming to compromises with them or, as in Voltaire's case, actually residing at a king's court – Rousseau's writings show no such readiness to compromise. He sums up this position clearly in his reply to the criticisms of his Discourse on the Arts and Sciences penned by the former King of Poland:

> The first source of evil is inequality. From inequality came wealth, for those words 'poor' and 'rich' are relative and everywhere that men are equal there are neither rich nor poor. [61]

If one did not know better, one would think that this was a quotation from Marx or Engels, who likewise saw the "original sin" of human history as consisting in the emergence of private property. Both Rousseau and Marx consider human history to have begun with a primitive society without private property. For Marx, the human race will eventually return, through the communist revolution, to this condition where all property is collective. Rousseau, however, did not draw any such conclusion. He considered it impossible to abolish the institution of private property once it had been established. For this reason the Marxists considered Rousseau's social theory to be inconsistent.

Of What Use Is Rousseau's Discovery for Us Today?

Rousseau's key demands for liberty, equality and fraternity have likewise become pillars of modern democracy. The equality of citizens before the law; compulsory free education; health insurance for all; free and universal suffrage – all these things might be argued to be consistent developments and applications of the attitude of mind first argued for by Rousseau.

But that part of Rousseau's heritage which is most binding upon us today is surely the moral duty not to allow history, in these respects, to slip backward. Today in Europe we see the gap between rich and poor once again growing larger. Access to education and better-paying professions is also once again becoming restricted to children from better-off households. It is incumbent on us here to defend the standards set by Rousseau already in the 18th Century and to hold high the banner of Enlightenment even amidst the rough winds of our late modern age. Even – indeed above all – in capitalist societies with competing actors in the marketplace free and equal access to opportunities for education and upward social mobility must remain a sacrosanct pillar of the social structure.

Daring More Democracy

Rousseau's demand for direct democracy and for regular popular assemblies in which the people themselves would decide on laws and on political lines to be followed remains, still today, an ideal toward which all, or most, democratic systems aspire. The Social Democratic German chancellor Willy Brandt spoke for many when he called on his country, at the end of the 1960s, to "dare more democracy".

In most presently-existing democratic systems laws and other key political decisions are passed by "representatives", for instance by elected members of parliament belonging to various parties. That this can mean a lack of citizens' real participation in these key decisions becomes particularly painfully clear when politicians fail to keep their promises to the electorate after being elected. Rousseau's critique of the British parliamentary system in 1762 remains astonishingly applicable still today:

The people of England believes itself to be free; it is quite wrong: it is free

Of What Use Is Rousseau's Discovery for Us Today?

only during the elections of Members of Parliament. Once they are elected, the people is enslaved, it is nothing. [62]

A democracy such as Rousseau envisaged – operating directly from the "base" of assembled citizens and dispensing with "representatives" or "deputies" – seemed, of course, for a long time to be materially impossible. It would be unfeasible, for example, to gather the whole population of France into a square to vote on every single law or policy. Rousseau himself conceded that his model of democracy could only work for very small states. His *Social Contract*, he was aware, represented only a kind of "thought experiment": democracy in its purest and most ideal form. As he wrote:

If the term is taken in its strict sense, true democracy has never existed and never will. [...] It is impossible to

> imagine the people permanently in session in order to deal with public affairs and it is easy to see that it could not set up commissions for the purpose without the form of administration being altered. [63]

Rousseau's scepticism about his own model of assemblies of all the people and direct democracy is understandable if one considers that there existed, in his day, not even loudspeakers or microphones to facilitate debate and the taking of a vote among a large number of assembled citizens.

But today much has become possible that formerly seemed utopian. It is feasible now in principle, thanks to Internet forums, blogs and other electronic media, for almost the entire citizenry to download drafts of laws, check them, discuss them, and come to a decision about them. Even in the Internet age, committees are still needed to formulate such drafts in legally appropriate language. But discussion of such draft laws, and votes on them, can nowadays indeed potentially be carried out directly by the people, in an "assembly of the whole citizenry" held in virtual form. In many European countries efforts are in fact already being made to allow citizens to vote directly, via plebiscites and referendums, on the use of atomic energy and other projects. Up until now such referendums have usually been held only on rare occasions and using conventional physical voting methods. But as we move deeper into the "virtual" age, with its rapidly growing technical possibilities, we are indeed seeing a vast renaissance of Rousseau's demand that the entire citizenry be directly participant in each political decision. There are many signs that our present parliamentary systems might give way, in the course of the coming century, to systems of direct democracy.

Mindfulness of Nature – Living Ecologically

It is sometimes maintained that Rousseau was the first "green" thinker: the founder of the modern movement toward environmental consciousness or, in other words, the first philosopher to have recognized the symbiosis existing between human life and Nature as a whole. There is certainly some truth in this. No other thinker pointed out so early in the modern age that Man needs to live in harmony with his natural environment. He warned against both the exploitation of Nature and the dangers of mass production. Astonishingly, we find him denouncing already in the mid-18th Century the adulteration and contamination of foodstuffs:

> If you think of the monstrous mixtures they eat, their pernicious seasonings, their corrupt foods and adulterated drugs, the cheating of those who sell such things […]

> and the poison in the vessels used for cooking; if you take note of the epidemic diseases engendered by the bad air where multitudes of men are gathered together […] you will see how dearly Nature makes us pay for the contempt we have shown for her lessons. [64]

Rousseau would surely be turning in his grave if he knew of the food-contamination scandals of today or could see the amount of traffic that passes, during rush-hours, through our big cities, with thousands

Of What Use Is Rousseau's Discovery for Us Today?

of workers squeezing themselves into subway trains, buying food and drink wrapped in plastic from fast-food restaurants and, having arrived in their open-plan offices, breathing recycled air from the air-conditioners and staring, motionless, all day long at computer screens.

There is no doubt that Rousseau would feel his critique of civilization to be entirely confirmed by today's world. We need now more than ever to be warned against the degradation of our foodstuffs. Genetically modified crops, microwaved fast-foods, pesticides in vegetables, "mad cow" disease and other scandals concerning the food on which we live would have outraged Rousseau as much as the dangerously degraded air-quality in our metropolises.

His warnings regarding population growth and urbanization have likewise gained rather than diminished in topicality. When the great Lisbon earthquake of 1755 took the lives of some 30,000 people, Rousseau wrote to Voltaire, saying:

> Admit that Nature did not assemble there twenty thousand houses of six to seven stories high and that if the inhabitants of

> that great city had been scattered more equally and housed more modestly, the damage would have been a lot less and perhaps none at all. ⁶⁵

One might apply today an argument similar to Rousseau's and point out that the tsunami which in 2011 destroyed large parts of the east coast of Japan would have caused far less damage if people had not built nuclear power plants on the coast near Fukushima. Rousseau was surely one of the first who urged mankind to try to calculate the negative consequences likely to follow from technical progress. He deplored, for example, the very harmful side-effects of industrial metal-production in his day:

> (Let) one add to all this the numbers of unhealthy trades which shorten lives or ruin men's physique – trades such as labouring in mines, various preparations of metals, minerals and especially lead, copper, mercury, cobalt, arsenic and realgar […]. ⁶⁶

If one takes all these observations regarding the exploitation of Nature together, there can be clearly made out an ecological conception at the core of Rousseau's work. Rousseau's central concern consisted in the demand that Man learn again to live in harmony with Nature. This meant a rejection both of our modern faith in technical progress and even of the exhortation that the Bible ascribes to God when it has Him tell Adam and Eve: "Fill the earth and subdue it." Rousseau was one of the first Western thinkers to understand Nature no longer in the terms suggested by this biblical passage – namely, as a hostile wilderness which needed to be "subdued" and cultivated – but rather as a teacher that could reveal to us the true interrelationships of life in the world. If we disturb the cycles and the harmony of Nature, we will pay a high price. Rousseau, as we have seen, plainly states that "Nature (already) makes us pay dearly for the contempt we have shown her." The explicit formulation "environmental sustainability" is, of course, not to be found in Rousseau's writing; but he was surely the first European representative of this stance. At the time, the demand that Man live in harmony with Nature seemed to be the eccentricity of a contrarian; but two hundred and fifty years later it has been recognized as a life-or-death issue for mankind.

Educating Man to be Free

The modern individual is in constant danger of absorbing his opinions only from others and of losing all trust in his own feelings. Rousseau recognized, already in the 18th Century, this immense pressure to conform:

> All our wisdom consists in servile prejudices. All our practices are only subjection, impediment and constraint. [67]

He passionately criticized every form of social coercion. This was why he saw the key task of education to be that of preventing children from becoming just "one of the herd" and helping them to become self-determined individuals. This idea too was considered comically eccentric by his contemporaries. But the idea of the natural self-realization of children was taken up again with great interest some two hundred years later, in the 1960s.

Under the slogan of "anti-authoritarian education" Rousseau's work became, during this decade, an inspiration for a movement of radical educational reform. Many parents belonging to the "counter-culture" of the day tried to raise their children without the use of punishment or coercion in any form. Spanking and caning, in particular, came to be seen as practices that had no place either at home or at school. Some even went so far as to allow their children to eat whatever food they preferred. It emerged, however, that this policy of encouraging unrestricted self-development in children not only often failed to produce the desired effects but was also unfeasibly strenuous for parents and teachers. As occurred with so many of the projects pursued with initial euphoria in the 60s, recent decades have seen the rise of a more moderate and realistic approach to children's "free self-development".

But even if "anti-authoritarian education" in this radical form had soon to be abandoned, many elements of Rousseau's philosophy of education remain a firm part of pedagogical doctrine. It is not just at "independent" schools and kindergartens, such as the Waldorf Schools, that children's self-development remains a key concern. Even state schools try nowadays to adapt their teaching to the child's own natural stages of maturation and the attempt is also made to promote those concrete, practical experiences thematized by Rousseau as a way of developing each child's individual talents.

Rousseau's far-sighted call for children to be allowed more freedom of movement is also recognized today as a very valid concern. It must not be forgotten that Rousseau's age favoured very strict methods of upbringing. Newborn children were literally sewn into swaddling-clothes so as to prevent them from wriggling – not only for fear of them injuring themselves but also to accustom them from early on to the still, obedient postures that would be required of most people not just as children but even as adults. Rousseau was, very rightly, critical of such measures:

> Civil man is born, lives and dies in slavery. At his birth he is sewed in swaddling clothes; at his death he is nailed in a coffin.

Of What Use Is Rousseau's Discovery for Us Today?

> So long as he keeps his human shape he is enchained by our institutions. [68]

This passionate warning against lifelong confinement in one or another kind of "swaddling" is another legacy of Rousseau's that we should never forget. Not just accepted educational and child-rearing practices but all social rituals and social compulsions in general must be examined and re-examined with a view to whether they really promote the healthy development of human beings.

Escaping the 'Matrix' – Living with Intensity

Although the Europe of Rousseau's day was still largely agricultural, industrial production, company competition and the complex taxation and banking system that go with these things already existed in embryonic form. Rousseau recognized this emergent capitalism and warned also of the negative effects it might have on mankind. He contrasted the statesmen of antiquity with those of the modern age, writing that:

> Ancient politicians spoke incessantly about mores and virtue; ours speak only of commerce and money. [...] They value men the way they would herds of cattle. According to them a man is worth no more to the state than what he consumes. [69]

Long before such Marxist critics of the "consumer society" and the "culture industry" as Marcuse and Adorno, Rousseau warned against the dangers of a total manipulation. He argued that the constant pursuit of money and prestige tends to submerge Man's true nature and replace it with an artificial "human nature", the nature of the "conspicuous consumer":

Of What Use Is Rousseau's Discovery for Us Today?

> (The) attentive reader […] will explain how the soul and the human passions through imperceptible degeneration change, so to speak, their nature; explain why our needs and our pleasures change their objects in the long run; and why, since original Man has disappeared by degrees, society no longer offers to the eyes of philosophers anything more than an assemblage of artificial men and factitious passions […]. [70]

Rousseau urges us to break out of the 'Matrix'-like false reality of this artificial world and to become mindful again of our inner, original nature. This exhortation, indeed, to break out of the 'false reality' of the modern world is the basic idea that runs through and animates Rousseau's whole body of work.

Already in his first essay for the Dijon Academy on "civilized" Man's increasing moral and physical degeneracy he had deplored the distortion of our originally healthy and uncorrupted nature by luxury, vanity and envy.

In his second essay on the origin of inequality he had held consistently to this line and criticized capitalist society, based on property, as an artificial and thereby unjust institution. Human beings, argued Rousseau, are by nature all equal and all have the same right to the fruits of the earth. It was only with the emergence of private property and a money-based economy that people became divided into rich and poor, freemen and slaves, powerful and powerless.

In his third and politically most important book, the *Social Contract*, he develops this theme still further and attempts to sketch out an ideal ordering of society whereby each man can live in a state with others while still retaining his original nature and liberty. Since this is a society which has no kings, statesmen, parliaments, or parliamentary deputies and parties and which consists rather of citizens who decide their own societal destiny in citizens' assemblies, the people who make it up remain, in this respect, as free as in the "state of Nature".

In his last great work too, *Emile*, Rousseau's concern is solely with how to preserve the original nature and the free development of Man and protect these things against the corrupting influences of society and of society's conception of education. Because Rousseau was firmly convinced that every human being bears within him, by nature, a good soul. It is the natural development of this soul, not the paths that traditional education sets him on or wants to set him on, that is the true vocation of every young person:

Prior to the calling of his parents is Nature's call to human life. Living is the calling […]. 71

What does Rousseau mean by this? There proceeds from Nature a "calling" to a truly human life. In this brief sentence there inheres an enormous explosive force and at the same time a fatal contradiction – one which possessed Rousseau all his life and allowed him no peace right up until the hour of his death. Because, on the one hand, Nature does indeed, from the moment we are born, "call" us to live out our curiosity, pleasure and joy in life trustingly, uncalculatingly and with all our heart; but on the other hand, so much stands in the way of our doing this that we are necessarily disappointed, settle for less, adapt ourselves to reality and are likely in the end to give up all the hopes and ideals that we cherished in earliest youth.

Rousseau, then, confronts us here with all the tragedy of human existence. Nature bears us as free, inquisitive children needful of love; but we have then to struggle our whole lives long against restrictions, resistances and necessities, so that at some point this open, sensitive loving attitude to life and the world always gives way to an attitude of cold calculation and conformity to the daily functional imperatives of society. Material matters like work and housing, or even more external and superficial preoccupations like our social standing, our consumption of the latest goods, or the obsessions of the media, become our dominating concerns until finally we are indifferent to everything but our own petty-bourgeois egotism and provisions for our own security. Against all this Rousseau raised his voice, devoting his genius to keeping modern human beings mindful of their sole true "calling" – the calling to be, precisely, real and full human beings:

Of What Use Is Rousseau's Discovery for Us Today?

In the natural order, since men are all equal, their common calling is Man's estate and whoever is well raised for that calling cannot fail to fulfil those callings related to it. [72]

Bibliographical References:

1. Jean-Jacques Rousseau, The Social Contract, translated by Christopher Betts, Oxford World's Classics, 1994, p. 45.
2. Jean-Jacques Rousseau, The Collected Writings of Rousseau, translated by Christopher Kelly, Hanover and London, University Press of New England, 1995, Vol. 5, p. 575.
3. Jean-Jacques Rousseau, Discourse on the Sciences and the Arts in Basic Political Writings of Jean-Jacques Rousseau, translated by Donald A. Cress Hackett Publishing Company, Indianapolis/Cambridge, 1987, p. 5.
4. Jean-Jacques Rousseau, Discourse on Inequality, translated by Maurice Cranston, Penguin Books, 1984, London, p. 82.
5. Ibid. p. 85.
6. Ibid. p. 102 (translation slightly revised).
7. Ibid. p. 99.
8. Ibid.
9. Ibid. p. 92.
10. Ibid. p. 103.
11. Ibid. p. 165 (Note L on John Locke).
12. Ibid. pps. 102-103.
13. Ibid.
14. Ibid. p. 85.
15. Ibid. p. 112.
16. Ibid. p. 116.
17. Ibid. p. 114.
18. Jean-Jacques Rousseau, Discourse on the Sciences and the Arts in Basic Political Writings of Jean-Jacques Rousseau, translated by Donald A. Cress Hackett Publishing Company, Indianapolis/Cambridge, 1987, p. 4.
19. Ibid.
20. Jean-Jacques Rousseau, Discourse on Inequality, translated by Maurice Cranston, Penguin Books, 1984, London, p. 136.

21 Ibid. p. 109.
22 Ibid. p. 89
23 Ibid. p. 120.
24 Ibid. p. 121.
25 Ibid.
26 Ibid. p. 122.
27 Ibid. p. 136.
28 Ibid.
29 Ibid. p. 104.
30 Voltaire, letter to Rousseau, August 1755, cited in Miscellaneous Letters in The Portable Voltaire, translated by Ben Ray Redman, Penguin Books, New York, 1968, p. 493.
31 Rousseau, letter to Voltaire, June 1760, cited in Maurice Cranston, The Noble Savage, Jean-Jacques Rousseau 1754-1762 (Chicago University Press, 1991) pps. 29-30.
32 Ibid. p. 153.
33 Ibid. p. 78.
34 Ibid. p. 147.
35 Jean-Jacques Rousseau, The Social Contract, translated by Christopher Betts, Oxford World's Classics, 1994, p. 45.
36 Ibid. p. 55.
37 Ibid. p. 50.
38 Ibid. p. 127.
39 Ibid. p. 59.
40 Ibid.
41 Ibid. p. 123.
42 Ibid. p. 63.
43 Ibid. p. 137.
44 Ibid. p. 58.
45 Ibid.
46 Ibid. p. 138.
47 Ibid. p. 168.
48 Ibid. pps. 71-72.
49 Ibid. p. 166.
50 Ibid. pps. 63-64.
51 Ibid. pps. 167-168
52 Jean-Jacques Rousseau, Emile, or On Education, translated by Allan Bloom, Basic Books, New York, 1979, p. 93

53 Ibid., p. 37.
54 Ibid. p. 78.
55 Ibid.
56 Ibid. pps. 177-178.
57 Ibid. p. 120.
58 Ibid.
59 Jean-Jacques Rousseau, Discourse on the Sciences and the Arts in Basic Political Writings of Jean-Jacques Rousseau, translated by Donald A. Cress Hackett Publishing Company, Indianapolis/Cambridge, 1987, p. 2.
60 Jean-Jacques Rousseau, Emile, or On Education, translated by Allan Bloom, Basic Books, New York, 1979, p.94.
61 Observations by Jean-Jacques Rousseau of Geneva on the Reply Made to His Discourse in Rousseau on Philosophy, Morality and Religion, edited by Christopher Kelly, University Press of New England, Hanover, New Hampshire and London, 2007, p. 12.
62 Jean-Jacques Rousseau, The Social Contract, translated by Christopher Betts, Oxford World's Classics, 1994, p. 127.
63 Ibid. p. 101.
64 Jean-Jacques Rousseau, Discourse on Inequality, translated by Maurice Cranston, Penguin Books, 1984, London, p. 149.
65 Rousseau, letter to Voltaire, August 1756, cited in Mark Sydney Cladis, Public Vision, Private Lives: Rousseau, Religion and 21st-Century Democracy, Columbia University Press, New York, 2003, p. 95
66 Jean-Jacques Rousseau, Discourse on Inequality, translated by Maurice Cranston, Penguin Books, 1984, London, p. 151.
67 Jean-Jacques Rousseau, Emile, or On Education, translated by Allan Bloom, Basic Books, New York, 1979, p.42
68 Ibid. pps. 42-43
69 Jean-Jacques Rousseau, Discourse on the Sciences and the Arts in Basic Political Writings of Jean-Jacques Rousseau, translated by Donald A. Cress Hackett Publishing Company, Indianapolis/Cambridge, 1987, pps. 12-13
70 Jean-Jacques Rousseau, Discourse on Inequality, translated by Maurice Cranston, Penguin Books, 1984, London, p. 135

71 Jean-Jacques Rousseau, Emile, or On Education, translated by Allan Bloom, Basic Books, New York, 1979, p.41 (translation slightly revised).

72 Ibid.

Already published in the same series:

Walther Ziegler
Camus in 60 Minutes
ISBN 9783741227738

Walther Ziegler
Freud in 60 Minutes
ISBN 9783741227707

Walther Ziegler
Hegel in 60 Minutes
ISBN 9783741227677

Walther Ziegler
Heidegger in 60 Minutes
ISBN 9783741227752

Walther Ziegler
Kant in 60 Minutes
ISBN 9783741226373

Walther Ziegler
Marx in 60 Minutes
ISBN 9783741227691

Walther Ziegler
Platon in 60 Minutes
ISBN 9783741227615

Walther Ziegler
Rousseau in 60 Minutes
ISBN 9783741227622

Walther Ziegler
Sartre in 60 Minuten
ISBN 9783741227653

Walther Ziegler
Smith in 60 Minuten
ISBN 9783741227721

Coming soon in the same series:

Walther Ziegler
Adorno in 60 Minutes

Walther Ziegler
Arendt in 60 Minutes

Walther Ziegler
Bacon in 60 Minutes

Walther Ziegler
Descartes in 60 Minutes

Walther Ziegler
Foucault in 60 Minutes

Walther Ziegler
Habermas in 60 Minutes

Walther Ziegler
Hobbes in 60 Minutes

Walther Ziegler
Nietzsche in 60 Minutes

Walther Ziegler
Popper in 60 Minutes

Walther Ziegler
Rawls in 60 Minutes

Walther Ziegler
Schopenhauer in 60 Minutes

Walther Ziegler
Wittgenstein in 60 Minutes

The author:

Dr Walther Ziegler is academically trained in the fields of philosophy, history and political science. As a foreign correspondent, reporter and newsroom coordinator for the German TV station ProSieben he has produced films on every continent. His news reports have won several prizes and awards. He has also authored numerous books in the field of philosophy. His many years of experience as a journalist mean that he is able to present the complex ideas of the great philosophers in a way that is both engaging and very clear. Since 2007 he has also been active as a teacher and trainer of young TV journalists in Munich, holding the post of Academic Director at the Media Academy, an institute of higher education that offers film and TV courses at its base directly on the site of the major European film production company Bavaria Film.